NURTURING YOUR
Seeds

22 PRINCIPLES FOR MODELLING
YOUR CHILD

Olubunmi Awe

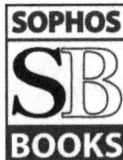

SOPHOS
SB
BOOKS

Nurturing Your Seeds
Copyright © 2017 by Olubunmi Awe

Published by
Sophos Books
163 Warbank Crescent
Croydon
CR0 0AZ

ISBN 978-1-905669-60-8

Cover design by *Icon Media*

Contents

Dedicated to my seeds,
Alpha, Emmanuel and Rhoda.

Love you all and thanks for supporting me
throughout the journey.

What a honour to be called your mother!

Author's Preface

This book was written in response to a burden that the Lord placed on me for young people. The more I spoke to these young ones and also considered how the Lord had helped me with my seeds, the burden to write only grew in proportion.

I have come to realise that we can pray for our children - and we cannot do without prayer! However, in addition to prayer, we can (and must) position our seeds for greatness. This involves intentional, proactive and deliberate effort.

These insights are tried and tested. I see results in my seeds daily, hence the urge to share with the world. *Nurturing Your Seeds* is not about raising the "smartest" child, but helping our children to become better day by day; guiding them to take those little steps that produce gigantic results; inspiring them daily through the words and actions to choose and follow the right path.

When we start the nurturing process early, the results will last!

I want to say thank you to all the families, children and young people that I spoke to, who allowed me to test them with this guide. And a special thanks to my children, who I am calling Super, Champion and Princess throughout the book.

I appreciate you all!

'Bunmi Awe

> *Children are the anchors that hold*
> *a mother to life*
>
> **- Sophocles**

PSEUDO NAMES USED IN THE BOOK

- Champion - Alpha
- Super - Emmanuel
- Princess - Rhoda

Foreword

It will take a miracle for a child to turn out well in a disjointed family or with a troubled background. Just as physical development requires eating the right kind of food, the spiritual, emotional and psychological growth of children in our care require deliberate steps that would mould them aright, which is referred to as *nurturing* in this book.

Olubunmi, the author is well-known to me. Over the years, I have observed her passion for the wellbeing of children and young adults, her desire to see them grow gracefully and her input into their lives aimed at making them better individuals. She has carried this burden over the years and has now penned it beautifully for all of us to benefit.

I echo the words of Frederick Douglass who said, "It is easier to build strong children than to repair broken men." The author, in this book, has emphasised the value and efficacy of early nurturing, which enables a viable, thriving and healthy society. She highlighted a wide range of issues, twenty-two in total, that have a bearing on how a child turns out in life and parents need to pay attention to. These include the power of spoken words, mind-set, the place and importance of the values of life, assigning chores and responsibilities and how these shape the life and future of a child. She took time to challenge parents, guardians and carers to be aware of the evil of hypocrisy and double standards, and to live as role models for those in their care. She also addressed the cankerworm of absentee parents that has eaten into today's homes, a syndrome of misplaced priorities.

I can go on and on! Simply, this must-read book is loaded! It is a timeless and timely treasure waiting to be unveiled. Nurturing your children and young people would be easier by the time you finish reading, whether as an older or a new parent!

Rev. Olayinka Bajomo
President, Lifesavers 47 (LISA)

Introduction

This book is not about how to raise "perfect" or robotic children. The notion of perfection is subjective, anyway. What is perfect to you is, perhaps, imperfect to someone else with differing values, from a different culture or environment. Our focus, instead, is to raise *unique* individuals who are perfected in Christ, taking it a step at a time because life itself is a process.

Children are my joy! I get on with them so easily and am always eager to see them grow positively. This requires careful and decisive nurturing with an end-goal in mind.

I love the definition of a seed, according to Collins Dictionary: "*The small*, hard part of a plant from which *a new plant grows*" (Emphasis mine).

Many people plant a seed and want to gather a harvest straight away. This will only lead to a premature seed. Between *the seed* and *the harvest* lies *the process*. Between the child and the mature adult are the formative years. As parents and carers (including god-parents, custodians, brothers, sisters, uncles, aunties and whoever is in charge of nurturing at any particular time), we have the privilege of depositing into the lives of children in our care.

The truth is, our input into their lives can be negative or positive, which goes a long way to impact their formation process. According to Oxford Dictionary, a process is defined as *"a series of actions or steps taken in order to achieve a particular end."*

The analogy of a seed (sperm) deposited into a woman, and the nine-month-long process it goes through before it enters this world as a bouncing baby, springs to mind. That process has to be completed to be called "full term." The same goes for a baby who later becomes a toddler, teenager, young adult and adult. The baby goes through a process! The child who goes to nursery school and later graduates from university has gone through some form of process years.

No child can come to full maturity without going through a successful developmental process and we who are custodians, keepers, guardians and protectors of these seeds will give an account to the Creator when the time comes.

TRUTH ABOUT YOUR SEEDS

Do you know that you are a carrier of greatness? Yes! And as a result of the greatness in you, your seed is great! When God created the earth, it contained the seeds that brought forth life. When He spoke and commanded the earth to bring forth plants, the earth did so because the seed was already there in creation (see Genesis 1).

God's Word never returns to Him void; according to Isaiah 55:10-12, it is like the rain and snow that cause the seeds to germinate and spring forth into their destiny. When God spoke, the seeds in the earth sprang to life.

In the same way, when God's Word comes to us, His truth waters our heart and causes the seeds of greatness in us to come to life!

The reason whey many do not realise that they carry seeds of greatness is because they have experienced many negative things happen and heard a lot of negative words spoken to them over the years. Do not believe a lie! You are loved and ordained by the Lord! He is the Lover of your soul.

God's plan and purposes for our lives (the seeds of greatness) are hidden deep within our being, waiting for the right words of life that would cause them to germinate.

Growth conditions must be exactly right before a seed can sprout. The temperature has to rise to just the right degree and there has to be sufficient light to beckon the seed to come forth. There is also one more ingredient that must be present to cause the seed to spring forth: WATER!

Water softens the shell that contains the seed so that the LIFE within the seed can BREAK OUT. Some even soak their seed in water before they are planted to ensure that they will germinate and grow properly.

I believe that the seeds of greatness God placed within us are waiting for the water of God's Word to bring them to life. Psalms 1:1-3 says that those who listen to God's Word and allow His truth to guide them shall become like TREES planted beside waters; and everything they do shall prosper. Your destiny contains greatness. God designed you that way.

I want you to catch a vision of greatness for the seeds in your care. Each of them are unique. Your seeds are fearfully and wonderfully created. They are perfect in God. They are a version of you: **"Mighty"** not "Mini"; **"Big"** not "Little". After all, you want them to do greater works than you have managed to do! (John 14:12).

Yet you have to nurture them lovingly if they will fulfil their God-given potential. The insights in the following pages will help you achieve this worthy goal. They include life principles, character-building disciplines and fun activities that would bring the best out of your seeds.

*Children are likely to live up to what
you believe of them*
- Lady Bird Johnson

1

Kindness to Others

One of the first life truths we need to impress upon our children is contained in the following Scripture: *"Treat others the same way you want them to treat you"* (Luke 6:31). It is the beginning of all other values. Not only should we teach it, we should also live it out before them. Children practise what we do and not just what we say.

I remember when I introduced this verse to my children. "If you want to be treated nicely," I told them, "then you have to treat others nicely." We even have a song for it (taken from Steve Green Memory Verse series).

My Super found this difficult to start with, but we kept reinforcing and explaining the importance of this principle to him. Our persistence paid off as he, of his own accord, put this down as one of his goals for the year! I was amazed that he did this. It showed me that he knew the value of treating others well. Although we are not there yet, we are taking it one step at a time! (For more on *Goal-setting*, see chapter 11).

I once asked him about his feelings when he got angry. We talked about this emotion and I helped him to manage his reactions. By engaging him, I was able to deposit truth inside him so that when it happened again, he would be able to gather his thoughts and remember how to respond.

It is easier to build strong children than to repair broken men.

- Frederick Douglass

2

What you think shapes what you see

Our thoughts come together to give us perspectives and attitudes through which we define and relate to the world around us. Arguably, nothing will hinder you in life as severely as a negative mind and a bad attitude. We can choose to feed our minds with thoughts that irritate us and make us miserable, or we can focus on thoughts that uplift us and make us feel good about life.

> "The mind is a set of cognitive faculties including consciousness, perception, thinking, judgement, and memory. The mind is the faculty of a human being's reasoning and thoughts." - Wikipedia

Our thoughts and minds are incredibly powerful, but our minds cannot distinguish between a real event and something we merely think about and believe. For instance, if you wake up from a nightmare, although it is not occurring in real life, your body will react physiologically with anxiety as if it were. The signals received by the brain are real, so the brain reacts as if it were real.

What does all this have to do with nurturing our children unto greatness? Here is the bottom line: Whatever picture you hold in your mind about your children is what they will ultimately manifest in real life. It does not matter what you say or pray; if in your heart of hearts, you think your child is not smart, that is what they will exhibit. Such is the power of the mind and thoughts. For your child to turn out as smart, your mind has to see that child as smart first. It is all about the mind.

Teach your seeds to know that their mind is powerful. Also, demonstrate the power of the mind before them through the words that you speak over them. Let your words flow out of the deep beliefs you have about your seeds.

Here are some positive words you can use when communicating with your children. How many of them do you use? Highlight them! Use them genuinely and see your children glow to do more.

POSITIVE WORDS:

- Thank you for your help.
- You should be proud of yourself!
- Look at your improvement!
- That "A" reflects a lot of hard work!
- You worked really hard to get this room clean!
- Thanks for helping set the table; that made a big difference.
- I noticed you were really patient with your little brother.
- What do you think about it?
- You seem to really enjoy science.
- Your hard work paid off!
- That's a tough one, but you'll figure it out.
- Look how far you've come!
- I trust your judgment.
- The time you're putting into your homework is really paying off.
- I love being with you.

- You really put a smile on her face with your kind words!

- That's coming along nicely!

- You really worked it out!

- That's a very good observation.

- Thank you for your cooperation.

- I see a very thorough job!

- That's what we call perseverance!

- I can tell you really care.

- You make it look easy!

- You've really got the hang of it!

- I can tell you spent a lot of time thinking this through.

- I really feel like a team when we work like this!

Children have never been very good at
listening to their elders,
but they have never failed to imitate them.

- James Baldwin

3

Values, Chores and Responsibility

Research has shown that children raised with clear values and who are given a sense of responsibility through assigned chores thrive better than those without such an upbringing. Values are not taught; they are caught. They shape children's character and develop their being. A child who lives in a house full of values shows wholesomeness in his or her development.

> *"Your values are your current estimations of truth. They represent your answer to the question of how to live."* - Steve Pavlina

Whether we are paying attention or not, our child's value system is being shaped everyday from a variety of sources: parents, friends, media, music, teachers, celebrities, advertisers, and experiences... (just to name a few). The importance of this truth cannot be overstated because the values that our children learn today will, in many ways, determine the type of life they will live as adults. Values will help shape their sense of right and wrong, their behaviours, their motivations, and how they choose to spend their money and time. Our child's tomorrow will be heavily influenced by the values they learn today.

It is of utmost importance, therefore, that we intentionally instil the right values into our children that will help bend their lives toward a positive future.

With this thought in mind, whether you are a parent or not, here is a list of values that children should treasure early in life above toys, sweets or any material possession.

Honesty

Children who learn the value and importance of honesty at a young age, have a far greater chance of becoming honest adults. And adults who deal truthfully with others tend to feel better about themselves, enjoy their lives more, and sleep better at night.

Family members

We work hard to teach our children about the importance of family. We look out for one another, care for one another, and cheer one another. Home is a safe place, a stable environment that provides the foundation for our children to succeed in life. A child who is proud of his family can always come home... no matter where life has taken him. This is so important!

Learning

Children need to value education. But more than that, they need to value the *process* of learning, so that they can become lifelong learners well beyond the years of formal education. Teach them to love reading, exploring, curiosity and how to ask good questions.

Their Soul

We have tried to instil into our kids that they are more than just flesh and blood taking up space. They are also made of mind, heart, soul, and will. The decisions they make in life should be based on more than just what everyone else with flesh and blood is doing;

their decisions should be based on the internal compass inside their heart and soul.

The Opposite Sex

Boys need to learn to value and respect girls. Girls need to learn to value and respect boys. Each offers unique insight and brings beauty into our world. Viewing the opposite sex in any other light leads to unhealthy relationships and ultimately, disaster.

Nature

Children who learn to appreciate the world around them develop the habit of caring for the environment. As a parent, I am frequently asking my kids to keep their rooms inside the house neat, clean and orderly. Shouldn't we also be teaching them to keep their world outside neat, clean and orderly?

Friendship

Good friends can be tough to come by, yet they can make all the difference in our lives. With the knowledge that honest, dependable and generous people attract honest, dependable, and generous friends, kids should learn from an early age to honour and care for their friends.

Determination

Life is full of challenges. It is important, then, to help children learn that not all problems will be solved quickly and easily. It will set them up to accomplish great things and keep dreaming and striving when others around them have already given up.

Quietness

In a world full of noise, valuing and enjoying quietness is a rarity. But solitude and meditation provides us the opportunity to self-evaluate our life, decisions, and direction. Successful people intentionally find room for quietness in their lives. Help your children to value time for thinking and unwinding.

Hard Work

Most people see hard work as just a means to an end. They work hard so they can earn a pay cheque. But hard work should be a reward in itself because not all hard work of lasting value is compensated handsomely. Help your children to enjoy hard work!

Justice

Life isn't fair! It never will be as there are just too many variables. But when a wrong has been committed or a playing field can be levelled, I want my child to be active in helping to level it… not hoarding power over another just to stay on top.

Art

Art represents the ability to create, communicate, and compel – three important actions for the rest of life. The importance of art in a society, a culture or an individual can never be overstated. It should always be valued and appreciated. For my children, art and music is therapeutic. It helps them to unwind.

Animals

Recognising the intrinsic value of animals helps children treat them with care and respect. Whilst this is an end in itself, treating animals with care and respect is an important step to treating other people with care and respect as well.

Affection

Love should not just be felt, it also needs to be expressed to be fully enjoyed and realised. Help your children to show affection without any sense of shame.

Themselves

Children who learn to value themselves are more likely to have self-confidence, self-esteem and self-worth. As a result, they are more likely to become adults who respect their values and stick to them, even when no one else is.

Truthfulness

Help kids find a way to tell the truth. The best way to encourage truthfulness in your child is to be a truthful person yourself.

Make Amends

Insist that children make amends especially if they know they are in the wrong. Get them to apologise (say sorry) for their wrongs.

Challenges

Encourage your children to take on a challenge. Never accept "I can't" from them. It is not about the winning; it's more about them trying. If they don't even try, how can they win? Remember it is a process. As an inventor, Edison made 1,000 unsuccessful attempts at inventing the light bulb. Edison's perspective was, "I didn't fail 1,000 times; *I have not failed. I've just found 1000 ways that won't work.*" Surely, that's the way to go!

CHORES AND RESPONSIBILITIES

What about chores? It is good practice to clearly assign chores and roles to children and help them embrace the responsibility of carrying them out. Studies show that involving **children** in household tasks at an early age **can** have a positive impact later in their life as they tend to be more successful in life.

According to the Guardian published on Sunday 15 November 2009 , Parents who don't give their children chores at home may be slowing their development; children should be given chores to help them develop a caring attitude and keep them grounded, according to a survey that found parents are now reluctant to ask children to do household tasks.

I must say that my children still forget sometimes, but I keep reminding them. Champion, for instance, does the trash and washing dishes on weekdays (Monday - Friday), while Super does it weekends. Champion does his laundry and ironing (I do the reminding!) etc. What am I getting at? Yes, there are days when the children have loads of homework and gladly chip in to help (Luke 6:31). Yet, I have seen families where children still have to do their chores whether they are doing exams or not. As long as this works in your home, it is fine.

Champion now makes us soup and you should see the joy in him when he completes it! He also prepares meals for his younger ones and even makes me food sometimes before I get home from work (that for me is showing care).

Instilling a sense of responsibility in your seeds will help them become accountable, which is a major skill in life for the future. They may not like it at the beginning, but they will thank you in the end. It also creates bonding and a sense of accomplishment once done!

The soul is healed by being with children

- Fyodor Dostoyevsky

4

Learning outside of the classroom

The era of "do as I *say*" is well over and the emphasis now is "do as I *do*." It is high time parents start practicing what they say. This is profound as we would always see a bit of what we do in each child.

I remember my god-daughter would call her dad "baby" because she saw her mum call him that so many times. As she grew up, she thought "Baby" was her dad's name! That is superb! But what of if she heard her father being called "foolish" (as I have heard some call their partners)?

What do you call your friends, seeds and the people around you? Your seeds are picking up traits from you, either good or bad. If you are a fearful person, chances are your seeds are growing up to be timid.

There is power in the words that we speak, and we will give an account for each word. If you manifest fear, you will see timidity in your seed; if you manifest confidence, they will copy you. So, let us build our children up with the right fruit of the Spirit, ***love, joy, peace, forbearance, kindness, goodness, faithfulness, gentleness and self-control.***

"But I tell you that everyone will have to give account on the Day of Judgment for every empty word they have spoken."

Matthew 12:36 NIV

"The soothing tongue is a tree of life, but a perverse tongue crushes the spirit."

Proverbs 15:4 NIV

"When there are many words, transgression is unavoidable, But he who restrains his lips is wise."

Proverbs 10:19 NIV

"For by your words you will be acquitted, and by your words you will be condemned."

Matthew 12:37 NIV

"The tongue has the power of life and death, and those who love it will eat its fruit."

Proverbs 18:21 NIV

NOW THINK: What habits have my seeds picked up from me and my partner? What would I like to change for the better? Write it down and start working on it... one day at a time!

Each day of our lives we make deposits in the memory banks of our children

- Chuck Swindoll

5

Communication and

Accessibility

The need to engage with and be available to children cannot be over-emphasised. I must say that this is a missing link in society right now. Too many parents are not accessible to their children. Sadly, a lot of children are not getting the first love required from the home, hence the need to get outside approval from anyone who would give it.

It is a common error of misplaced priority when parents relinquish their nurturing responsibilities to a system, teacher, school, church or another person. I am a strong believer in the adage that "it takes a village to raise a child;" notwithstanding, our seeds need validation and affirmation first from home. This brings a joy that cannot be quantified; it helps a child to thrive in any environment knowing they are loved and accepted.

Remember, it is your duty to help your seeds realise their full potential. So, share ideas with them. Chat with them about things that happened in your childhood that made you laugh as a child. You will be surprised that the things we consider little are the things that make their world, not the gadgets and toys that bring only temporal happiness.

Be there for your children anytime, anywhere. Let them know they can always come to you for anything - and I mean ANYTHING!

I share with my children childhood stories, things that happened to me while I was in the boarding house, and they laugh. I even teach them some of my childhood songs and all of these make them ask more questions.

I remember when Champion wanted to ask me questions on sex and I was about to make dinner. I left everything immediately to talk to him, as I knew if I postponed it, he might not be as interested in the topic as before. It is more about quality time, not quantity.

I once saw the caption below on Facebook (*author unknown*):

> *"Talk to your daughters*
>
> *Play with your sons*
>
> *You need to better friend to them than anyone else. The society offers lots of evil friends/ options. Before they make those kinds of friends, they need to find their best friend in YOU!"*

Simple things like playing music, telling stories or singing songs can make all the difference between mundane tasks and family fun time.

Again, it is about **quality** time not **QUANTITY**! Create those lifetime memories for them now and for generations to come!

Live so that when your children think of fairness, caring, and integrity, they think of you

- H. Jackson Brown, Jr.

6

Praying and Pointing them to the Father

Do you pray for your seeds? Everyone does, right? But, do you intentionally set time aside to fast and pray for them? We are spirit beings and we should command the atmosphere, air, water, stars, moon, land and sky to work in favour of our seeds.

Just as we project and strategise in life, we must plan for our children spiritually and pray for them intentionally. We must also protect them and point them to their heavenly Father. He has the plan and purpose for their lives

Through prayer, you can give them a generational, godly inheritance that they can also pass down to generations after them. This is the most important inheritance one can pass down to the next generation.

> "A good person leaves an inheritance for their children's children, but a sinner's wealth is stored up for the righteous."
>
> **Proverbs 13:22**

> "And that you may tell in the hearing of your son, and of your grandson, how I made a mockery of the Egyptians and how I performed My signs among them, that you may know that I am the LORD."
>
> **Exodus 10:2**

> "We will not conceal them from their children, But tell to the generation to come the praises of the LORD, And His strength and His wondrous works that He has done."
>
> **Psalm 78:4**

We must speak to our seeds about the wonders that God has done in our lives. Set up an Ebenezer in your home. I remember early on in our marriage, that my hubby was troubled about an issue. I simply took a pen and paper and wrote down what I know the

Lord has done, even to the minute details of how much He has been our refuge (including life, air, sanity etc.). I posted this to my hubby via mail as we can easily forget these blessings, especially when we are passing through challenges. I said in the letter that if the Lord has indeed done these, He can do all things; and even if it is not done yet, we will rejoice in our waiting. Amen!

My hubby saw the letter and turned to the Lord in thanksgiving. The enemy cannot steal our joy if we encourage ourselves in the Lord always!

I periodically let my children know when God comes through for us and what He has done in the past. Hence, whenever they have issues, they go directly to their Father and then to us, the earthly parents. They are still growing and learning daily.

I pray that the Lord will give us the strength in this area because the world is also pulling, but in the end, our children are of the Lord's and great shall be their reward in Jesus name.

> "All your children will be taught by the LORD, and great will be their peace."

Isaiah 54:13

Many seeds go to church, but the question is: do they have a relationship with the Lord? This is very important because there would be days when we are not there and stuff happens. Would they wait on you or call God themselves? They have so many books but do they have their Bible as well?

Start with a chapter a day and a verse a week (this works for me). Do whatever works for you as long as it is done consistently. The idea is not competition, but a personal relationship with their Daddy in heaven. So, when they have a bad dream, they would have prayed before they come to you.

Let your children see Christ in you. Indeed, charity should start at home.

> "We will not hide them from their children, but tell to the coming generation the glorious deeds of the Lord, and his might, and the wonders that he has done. He established a testimony in Jacob and appointed a law in Israel, which he commanded our fathers to teach to their children, that the next generation might know them, the children yet unborn, and arise and tell them to their children, so that they should set their hope in God and not forget the works of God, but keep his commandments; and that they

should not be like their fathers, a
stubborn and rebellious generation, a
generation whose heart was not steadfast,
whose spirit was not faithful to God."

Psalm 78

There is so much within this text that we often miss. It does not say that the church is supposed to tell the coming generations of the deeds of the Lord; parents should. Discipleship is both initiated and cultivated in the home.

Parents have more influence than they can ever imagine when it comes to the spiritual development of their children. When children see faith displayed in the lives of their parents, they naturally will want to display those same qualities. Yet, the question that is asked by so many parents is, "Where do we begin with this seemingly daunting task?" I believe there are three things that can bring discipleship back into the home and make it a reality once again.

1. Parents must tell their children how they came to faith in Christ.

I can think of many children that have no idea how their parents came to know Christ. The children know that their parents believe in God. However, they are not sure what drew them into a relationship with Jesus. Your story of salvation is also a part of your child's story of salvation. Therefore, telling them how you met Jesus makes salvation a real thing to them.

The more they hear your salvation story, the more they are likely to experience their own story of salvation. It is one thing for a pastor to stand in the pulpit on Sunday mornings and talk about coming to faith in Christ. When children hear the story of how you came to faith in Christ, it becomes more meaningful to them. This allows the children to grasp what life is like without Christ, to realise their own lost-ness. But more importantly, they get to hear how Christ changed you and how you are now a new person. Through this, salvation becomes more real to them, which can lead to a continual spiritual conversation in the household.

2. Parents must take every opportunity to point to Christ.

We look for teaching moments in a child's life every day. However, these usually pertain to their behaviour rather than their spiritual development. God has blessed us with 6,408 days, from a child's birth to the 18th birthday, to continuously point our children to Him. If parents are the primary disciples of their children, then every moment can either point them to God or to the world.

We will do whatever it takes to make sure we have "good" kids that have "good" behaviour. However, our behaviour flows out of our heart. Therefore, issues of behaviour are truly a matter of the heart. Matthew 15:19 says, "But what comes out of the mouth proceeds from the heart, and this defiles a person." Luke 6:45 says, "The good person out of the good treasure of his heart produces good, and the evil person out of his evil treasure produces evil, for out of the abundance of the heart his mouth speaks." Jesus was telling his listeners that who we truly are comes from the heart. Moments of discipline are teaching moments pointing back to our belief in God. Therefore, we must understand that there is so much going on beneath what we see on the surface.

As parents, God has equipped us to speak directly into the heart of our children by pointing them to the Saviour, Jesus Christ.

3. Parents must show their children Jesus by the way they live.

This is the scary part, because if anyone knows that parents mess up, it is their children. They see the good, the bad and the ugly of their parents. However, parents can live a life that is pleasing to the Lord, and their children will follow suit.

I remember growing up and watching my parents love others in a way that had a huge impact on how I now treat others. I also remember seeing my parents being confronted by a person who was upset and agitated, and how they handled that person with so much grace and mercy. I am not at all saying that they were perfect; they did, however, model for me the fruits of the Spirit. They showed me that if Jesus truly lived in my life, then others will notice by the way I talk and by how I love others.

Sometimes, living out your spiritual life in front of your kids means admitting that you are a sinner too. This is scary, but whether you like it or not, your children know that you are not perfect. So, it is time to take down the mask and admit that you struggle with certain things. Just think about the impact it would have on a child who struggles with anger to sit down with their parent, and the parent explains how they handle life when they are angry. This would change the way kids understood their parents.

Psalms 127:3-5 says, *"Behold, children are a heritage from the Lord, the fruit of the womb a reward. Like arrows in the hand of a warrior are the children of one's youth. Blessed is the man who fills his quiver with them! He shall not be put to shame when he speaks with his enemies in the gate."* Children are a blessed gift from the Lord. Therefore, their spiritual development is of upmost importance to the family and to the church. God has called parents to be the primary disciples of their children and not the church. The church is called to journey alongside parents.

*The greatest sign of success for a teacher...
is to be able to say, 'The children are
now working as if I did not exist'*

- Maria Montessori

7

Obeying Authorities

It is important we teach our children to respect authority. Once we succeed in establishing the right values in them, and we have pointed to the Father, this would be easy for them to achieve. Authorities include their elders, school teachers, government, judges, police officers, the law etc. It is important that we groom this in them from when they are young so that when they grow older, they will not depart from it.

> "Everyone must submit to governing authorities. For all authority comes from God, and those in positions of authority have been placed there by God. So anyone who rebels against authority is rebelling against what God has instituted, and they will be punished. For the authorities do not strike fear in people who are doing right, but in those who are doing wrong. Would

you like to live without fear of the authorities? Do what is right, and they will honour you. The authorities are God's servants, sent for your good. But if you are doing wrong, of course you should be afraid, for they have the power to punish you. They are God's servants, sent for the very purpose of punishing those who do what is wrong. So you must submit to them, not only to avoid punishment, but also to keep a clear conscience. Pay your taxes, too, for these same reasons. For government workers need to be paid. They are serving God in what they do. Give to everyone what you owe them: Pay your taxes and government fees to those who collect them, and give respect and honour to those who are in authority."

Romans 13:1-7

"So they brought it, and He asked them, 'Whose likeness is this? And whose inscription?' 'Caesar's,' they answered. Then Jesus told them, 'Give to Caesar what is Caesar's, and to God what is God's.' And they marvelled at Him."

Mark 12:17-19

The greatest gifts you can give your children are the roots of responsibility and the wings of independence

- Denis Waitley

8

Understanding Success

is for them

Success means different things to different people. For some, it means the acquisition of material things; while for some, it is touching another life positively; yet others attribute success to when their children get good grades. What is success to you? Write it down!

For the purpose of this book, I will define success simply as a step better than yesterday in anything we do; or the gradual steps towards the accomplishment of an aim or purpose. In other words, success is not just an accomplishment, but also the gradual steps towards the accomplishment. Success, defined in this way, is holistic. It allows us to celebrate each milestone along the way.

Take the example of the accomplishment of graduating from the university. The equally important milestones will include going to nursery, tuition classes, primary, secondary, college, values, skills etc. - everything that helped to shape this child into a university degree holder. Finishing at the University is not the only success that should be celebrated; the number of years that contributed to this milestone have to be eminent too.

We should also celebrate and praise our children when they make attempts at anything. My Super always says, "At least I tried. I may not have won but I tried." That for me is success because if you stop trying, you cannot win!

Let your children know that they may not win some times, and that it is okay to celebrate those who win!

Every child is an artist. The problem is how to remain an artist once he grows up

- Pablo Picasso

9

Gifts, Talents and

Opportunities

Every child has a blueprint of his life and as parents, you can help to birth them into their purpose. Watch out for when they display their skills, gifts and talents; do not be too carried away that you miss it!.

> "I praise you because I am fearfully and wonderfully made; your works are wonderful, I know that full well. My frame was not hidden from You, When I was made in secret, And skilfully wrought in the depths of the earth."
>
> **Psalm 139:14-15**

"Before I formed you in the womb I knew you, before you were born I set you apart; I appointed you as a prophet to the nations."

Jeremiah 1:5

Have a journal for your children. Write things down for each one (be accountable); nurture their gifts daily. Each child is an individual, specially made for a unique purpose. Enter them into competitions and if they do not win, at least they tried (See "Get them ready for the real world"). Let them know that success is a process and the ability to try is also part of the process.

If they have a skill in an area, help them to develop it. Showcase them to the world when opportunities present themselves (as this is a strength for them, it means they are naturals in this area and will enjoy it). Take pictures of them displaying their talents and abilities, especially when they are young and do a keepsake.

I once read somewhere that you can open an email and send all of these pictures there, waiting to present it to them at 18 – a very good idea!

I remember the first time Champion told me he wanted to play football. I refused because it was going to collide with church attendance on Sundays. Thank God for the timely *KingsGen Parenting Conference*, where a gentleman, Bola the Builder, spoke on this subject (an Economist turned Builder, who is now an entrepreneur). It was as if he spoke directly to me. He asked this question: Is it only on Sundays that a child goes to church? Is that child's foundation in Christ shaky? I asked myself these questions and realised that Youth Services were held twice weekly (Fridays and Sundays) and Champion loved going. So, I said to him, "Whenever you have tournaments on a Sunday, make sure you go to Youth Service on Friday." He gladly accepted!

He is now enjoying his football, as well as doing other things with joy because this is a gift for him that must be nurtured. As for me, all I can see is a busy and focused lad!

Parents let's not be too rigid in the way we do things. Be ready to learn, unlearn and re-learn!

Give me four years to teach the children and the seed I have sown will never be uprooted

- Vladimir Lenin

10

Homework and Exams

Homework is normally given to a child to check how well they understand a topic that has been taught. It also helps you as a parent to know your child's strength and weakness, and help them overcome any shortcomings.

Parents are not to do their children's homework for them. You can explain or remind them with another example, but you must get them to do their homework themselves.

I must stress here that a lot depends on the age of the child. With wisdom and tact, you can also introduce the concept of independent learning to your children.

For instance, when my 8-year-old asks me for the meaning of a word, I ask him, "When we do not understand the meaning of a word, where do we go to check it up?"

He would look at me and say, "Mum, just tell me the meaning!"

If I tell him the meaning just to make things quick and easy, I am not teaching him in the long run. For this reason I refuse to tell him. Instead, I tell him, "Go get yourself a dictionary!"

What this does is to help him know where to go to get help the next time, even when mum is not around. He understands this concept. The other day, he wanted to know more about Prepositions. He went to YouTube and typed the word and learnt from the tutorials on Prepositions!

They need to know that homework is not for the parents to do. Their achievements in school work should be theirs. In other words, they should *own* their success, with parents only helping to steer them in the right direction.

For some children, homework is a struggle. If your children are struggling in this area, I highly endorse John Rosemond's book, titled *Ending the Homework Hassle*. Rather than mere tips and tricks for homework hassles with your kid, this book teaches PARENTS on how to better guide their children, so children magically start accepting their responsibilities, which in the end prepares them for responsible adulthood. The more you hound, 'hover' over and check on them, the more you worry for them, and the less they do themselves, which progressively makes them more dependent on you and less on themselves.

This theory took me by surprise, as I wanted to be extremely involved with my child's work in school. But, I had no idea I was actually hindering their growth and understanding of responsibility and accountability. The book also offers help for parents and children with consistent homework problems, attitudes, and resistance. It's an excellent and easy-to-read book. I highly recommend it!

Hugs can do great amounts of good - especially for children

- Diana, Princess of Wales

11

Goal-Writing for Clear Direction

Goal-setting is an important exercise for deciding what you want to achieve in your life. It involves having short and long-term goals and working towards them in chunks, hereby separating what is important from what is irrelevant. This could be done in different areas of life, including physical and spiritual wellbeing, academics, relationships, faith etc.

It is one thing to set goals and another thing to achieve them. This is why goals that are worth pursuing must be SMART - a well-known acronym that guides the setting of goals. In other words, your goals must be:

S - Specific

M - Measurable

A - Achievable

R - Realistic

T - Timely

Guiding our children to set SMART goals is, therefore, the first step in making their goals a reality. It helps to motivate them and build their self-confidence. As they achieve their short-term goals, the success would spur them on to the next goal. Even if they do not achieve it, they can carry it over to a new timeline. Adults do this, so why not help child develop this skill from when they are young so that when they are old, they will not depart from it?

I also make them see my goals (practising what I preach!), and in the mid-year, review my goals openly for them to see.

Goal-writing also includes what the Lord has spoken to you concerning your children; He speaks on each one and what He says is different from one to the other as they are uniquely made.

Just like the story of Joseph who had a dream, your children will have dreams and they will come to you- please write them down as they will come to pass. If there are any not-so-good-ones, pray against them.

> "Take a scroll and write on it all the words which I have spoken to you concerning Israel and concerning Judah, and concerning all the nations, from the day I first spoke to you, from the days of Josiah, even to this day."
>
> **Jeremiah 36:2**

DO WE REALLY FORGET?

Many people have concluded that the human mind is too complex to explain, and memory is no exception. Although vast amounts of research have been carried out into how we remember (and forget!) things, nobody knows for sure the model on which human memory is based.

There are, nonetheless, two main reasons for which psychologists think we 'forget' information:

You store information in your memory but are unable to remember it when you need to, but perhaps can at a later date. In this case, information is *inaccessible*.

The human memory simply forgets

information, permanently, and the physical traces of the memory disappear. In which case, information is *unavailable*. The solution, therefore, is to write your goals for the sake of future reference.

> "Then the LORD replied: "Write down the revelation and make it plain on tablets so that a herald may run with it."

Habakkuk 2:2

I started goal-writing exercises with my children when my first was 7 years old. I thought, if adults write their goals, why not children too? It started quite awkwardly, but it is not so anymore. Champion now writes goals effortlessly and Super now does it too, having seen this modelled time and time again.

The children's goals should come from the children (this is important) and not what mummy or daddy wants, as this is the main essence of enabling the children to think for themselves. It can be as simple as, "I want to get better in Maths." You can respond by asking, "Now, how can you get better in Maths?" To which they may answer, "By spending 10 minutes a day on my Maths." Your job as a parent is to help them break down their goals into smaller chunks.

Some of the goals that Champion wrote for this term (we review half term) was: Behaviour, 2+ (he wanted his behavioural ratio in school to move up a level). We could have written 1+ but had to work with him to 2+ first; afterwards, 1+ would be easily achievable.

Another goal that Champion set was learning how to make okro soup. He had already achieved the goal of making chicken stew for the family; now he wanted to learn okro soup! He wrote this down while I was making the soup and now it was time for him to try it out. We were ready to joyfully eat whatever he made together knowing it would get better the next time!

Another goal Super wrote was to "Control anger." We sat down and asked him how this can be done as he gets angry easily. Talking about these issues helped because his anger management got better. Whenever he feels provoked, he remembers the family talk.

VISION BOARDS

Whenever my children set goals, I encourage them to write them out and place them in their rooms, alongside their daily affirmations. It is helpful that they see their goals everyday. We also have a vision board for the family, where each child's vision is clearly displayed.

A vision board is a tool used to clarify and maintain focus on specific life goals. Literally, a vision board is any sort of board on which you can display images that represent whatever you want to be, do or have in your life.

On this board, we have what each child will be (which may change as they get older), schools they will go, income goals and aspirations for the family, spiritual and economic goals etc. We also have each child's picture on the board, which helps us to be focused as what we see and speak about, we attract. But most importantly, the children are inspired to work towards their goals on the vision board.

For example, to say "I want a better life" is a fine goal, but have you given serious thought to exactly what that means? Try to envision what your "better life" looks like. For those of us who find that somewhat difficult, making a *vision board* can be a tremendous help.

In order to create my vision board, I must actively seek images that represent specific details of this wonderful new life. That means narrowing it down to specifics.

For some, a better life might mean having a new car or home.

Others may be seeking a new relationship or improvements in existing relationships. Perhaps you have heard it said that most of us never get what we want because we don't know what we want. Making a vision board is a wonderful way to bring clarity to that general desire and turn it into an achievable goal. Vision boards can also include words, phrases or sentences that affirm your intentions.

TIPS FOR CREATING A VISION BOARD

Here are a few tips for you to create a vision board for your family.

Material:

Any kind of board would do. If you have not created one before, perhaps start with a cork board or poster board from the hardware store. I recommend a pin board or something pretty you would be pleased to look at.

You would also need scissors, tape, pins and, if necessary, glue-stick to put your board together. If you want, you can get fun markers, stickers or anything else you can think of to deck out your board. I don't use any of these stuff, but if embellishments make you feel great, then go for them!

You can cut images or quotes from magazines or print them out from the internet. Get as many artefacts as possible, even if you do not use them all: photos, quotes, sayings, images of places you want to go, reminders of events, places, or people, postcards from friends and just about anything that will inspire you.

Time:

Give yourself a stress-free hour or two to put your board together. Get all the family together and make a party of it! We hold a vision board party every year and goes a long way to set the tone for the year. Everyone is more focused and less stressed after we do it.

Process:

Set the mood. Turn off the TV and turn on some relaxing music. Light a candle and clear your space.

When it comes to actually putting your stuff on the board, I like to leave space between each item because clutter clouds my mind. However, if you love the feeling of closeness and want everything to touch and overlap, then huddle it all together and overlap your objects. As for choosing what makes the final cut, lay everything out before you start gluing and pinning so you can get an idea of where you want everything.

What do you think? Will you create a vision board if you don't have one already? I hope the answer is yes!

You can learn many things from children.
How much patience you have, for instance

- Franklin P. Jones

12

Media Exposure

The media is a major feature in the everyday life of families today. By "media," I am referring to all forms of mass communication: broadcasting, publishing and the world wide web. Examples include billboards, television, books, music and social media etc. I must stress here that the media is neither good nor bad. It is rather neutral. It is what you do with it that matters.

It goes without saying that parents need to monitor their children's activities on and engagement with the media. They need to be aware of what their children *see* and *hear* - the two important gateways that shape our minds.

Monitoring your children's media activity does not necessarily mean banning them from the TV or internet (which could work when they are little and you are in charge of everything); it is more important that you explain to them what this is all about. Engage them in a balanced discussion and help them to understand the various implications of media exposure.

During a Bible study session at home, we considered the reasons why Samson lusted after Delilah, and how David lusted after Bathsheba. The common factor in both situations was the enticing information that came into their heart through their eyes. Both of them could have avoided falling into sin if they guarded their heart and eyes. Our seeds need to know that they are in control of what enters their heart through their eyes and ears; that they can ask the Holy Spirit for help in every way and He will come to their aid.

How these "little foxes" spoil the vines! How they rob our lives of the fruit that the Holy Spirit is waiting and wanting to produce in and through us! We need to deal with them before they deal with us!

Don't worry that children never listen to you; worry that they are always watching you

- Robert Fulghum

13

Peer Pressure

Peer pressure is a real issue that young people face everyday. Mostly, it is viewed from a negative standpoint. However, I want to simply define it as influence from members of one's peer group, which can be positive or negative. There is good pressure - for instance, peers studying together and stretching one another's academic capabilities; there is also bad pressure - for instance, a child being bullied by other children.

It is important we let our children know that they are not supposed to bully other children.

Bullying or negative pressure should also not come to them and when a child gets you into their world and lets you know this, never take it for granted and act on this information through more information, questions and in the end report this!

Also, make sure that we talk to our children as unfortunately how ugly this may sound, they could be the bully; let them know the impact and risk of this and how important this issue is.

Negative peer pressure can sometimes lead to drugs, Alcohol, Smoking, Bullying and unfortunately death in some circumstances.

Let's help STOP this by educating our seeds and building, nurturing, validating long term relationships with them! If it must be, it's up to US!

A child who is allowed to be disrespectful to his parents will not have true respect for anyone

- Billy Graham

14

Keep it Simple and Sincere
(KISS)

*K*eep *it simple* was a phrase that Dr. Bob used in the early days of AA to remind Bill Wilson that too much information was destructive for the newcomer. What he really meant, in my opinion, was "Let's stay focused." This has been changed to Keep It Simple and Sincere!

As you devote time to nurturing your children, kindly keep things simple, depending on your child's age and ability. You know your child well. I advise you to work with your seed wherever they are and whenever the time is available. Don't be too pushy with your children. Take it one day at a time and it will end in praise!

Also, stop comparing your children with others; rather, celebrate your children and help them. You are their help and trust and if you don't do it for them, nobody will!

When you see a child of the same age with yours and you are privileged to see what they know, appreciate yours as there are many who are out there who would love to be in your own shoes so be thankful and KISS.

Children are like wet cement.
Whatever falls on them makes an impression

- Haim Ginott

15

Know their Friends

Most people underestimate the power of association. Their choice of who they associate with is driven primarily by convenience and circumstance. The people that we spend time with will impact on our thinking greatly. Show me your friends, it is said, and I can tell you who you will become in a few years!

This will be evident in the lives of our seeds.

> Do not be misled: "Bad company corrupts good character."
>
> **I Corinthians 15:33**

"One who has unreliable friends soon comes to ruin, but there is a friend who sticks closer than a brother."

Proverbs 18:24

"Do not make friends with a hot-tempered person, do not associate with one easily angered, or you may learn their ways and get yourself ensnared."

Proverbs 22:24-25

"For each tree is known by its own fruit. For men do not gather figs from thorns, nor do they pick grapes from a briar bush."

Luke 6:44

There are weeds (friends) that need to be uprooted from the lives of our seeds. Do this as soon as they become noticeable. Start uprooting through prayer and also apply godly wisdom.

Ask your children questions about their friends and get to know them well. In most cases, they are likely to be a replica of your seeds, as like begets like!

If you hang around 5 confident people, you will be the 6th!

If you hang around 5 successful people, you will be the 6th!

If you hang around 5 idiotic people, unfortunately you will be the 6th! (Ouch!).

You cannot hang around negative people and expect to live a positive life

- Joel Osteen

You are the average of the 5 people you spend your time with

– Jim Rohn

16

Sex Education

Our children are growing in a world that openly displays sex-related imagery and actively seeks to influence young minds in particular view points. For these reasons and more, we cannot sway sex matters to a corner. You cannot afford to relinquish your responsibilities to the school, youth leaders, friends or the media.

My hubby and I chat regularly with our children on sex issues. What we say and how deep we go depends on the age of the child. If you have never done this before, it is better later than never! The first time might feel awkward, but do not shy away from it. If you do not talk about sex, they will discuss it when you are not there, with people you may not approve of.

You do not need to make sex a big issue. Discuss it anytime, anywhere, especially when you feel a nudge to do so - you know your child the best!

It matters where your children first hear about sex. This first discussion is so important. In my opinion, it is better they first hear about sex from you, their custodian! My Champion now comes home and discusses this subject with me, casually asking questions whenever the school teaches on it. He is able to ask me because we have created an open and conducive atmosphere for it.

WHAT IN THE WORLD IS HAPPENING?

"Or do you not know that your body is a temple of the Holy Spirit within you, whom you have from God? You are not your own, for you were bought with a price. So glorify God in your body."

I Corinthians 6:19-20

"But I say, walk by the Spirit, and you will not gratify the desires of the flesh."

Galatians 5:6

It really baffles me when I consider what is going on in the hearts of many young people today. Why have young girls become so assertive? I think there are several reasons for what we are seeing.

First, the culture is supporting sexual awareness. Movies, television shows, commercials, magazines, books, pop music, the internet... they all glamorise sex and intimacy. They encourage and promote the right of young women to go after whatever they think will make them happy.

Secondly, we have a whole generation of young men who are confused in their own sexual identity. Are they supposed to be sensitive or aggressive? Leaders or helpers? Many young men today are not being taught how to treat young ladies with nobility, dignity, and respect. Many are growing up without a father or male figure to provide guidance. As a result, they have no expectation of how a young lady should treat them.

Thirdly, the breakdown of the family has resulted in a whole generation of daughters who have been abandoned. And in the absence of a healthy, emotional attachment to their fathers and mothers, they're trying to fill their emotional gas tanks with the opposite sex.

Finally, there's little or no preparation for adolescence occurring among parents of pre or early teens. This may be the core problem. When you ask parents of preteens how many of them would like their children to have the same experience they had in adolescence, only a few hands will go up. But these same parents often become increasingly detached as their children move into the adolescent years.

TEACH ABSTINENCE

As you hold standards up for your teenage children, be sure to explain some of the reasons God commanded us to abstain from sexual immorality, including freedom from guilt, emotional scars, and comparison; freedom from sexually-transmitted diseases and unwanted pregnancies; and preservation of a gift that can only be given to one person. God surely has our best interests in mind.

Today, parents need the courage of David to face "Goliath" called sex. When it comes to discussing sexuality with our children, we may feel like a boy with five smooth stones running into battle against a huge monster. But David ran toward the giant. He met him head on in battle and defeated him.

What was the key to David's courageous action? His faith in God. Likewise, as parents, we need to walk by faith and take action with courage. You can do it!

PROTECTING YOUR BOYS

There are six assumptions you need to make when training and educating your sons on how to handle aggressive girls.

Assumption #1

Young boys are clueless about a lot of things that is going on around them.

Boys need to be prepared for the reality of today's world, and this preparation needs to start while they are still young. This is why I suggest that mothers and fathers talk with their 10- to 12-year-old sons about how they relate to the opposite sex before they face the temptation. There's a much greater probability of success if you can have these conversations before the hormones hit.

Assumption #2

Aggressive girls will likely come into your son's life.

The problem is that most parents would not be aware of it, because teenage boys hardly talk about anything! It could be taking place in your son's life and he's just not letting you know. So, you have to pursue him in the process.

Assumption #3

You, as a parent, need a proactive plan. That plan will involve fathers and sons, but ...

Assumption #4

Mums, that plan needs to involve you. You know how girls think and you can help your son understand girls in ways that a father can't.

Assumption #5

With a son, this instruction, teaching, and call to accountability does not end with the adolescent years. It continues on into adulthood. It does not stop after they get married. Why? Because there are women who are still preying upon men who are married and every man needs an older man in his life who can keep him accountable.

Assumption #6

Your son needs a call to manhood. Ultimately, the call to a young man is to step up and become a noble man, a moral man, a spiritual man, God's man. You are going to call your sons as they move through adolescence to step up to maturity and real manhood. And to attain that, they need a mother and father teaching Scripture and encouraging them as they take these steps toward maturity.

One of the finest illustrations of this is in Proverbs, Chapters 5-7. In this passage, the writer was reflecting on conversations he had with his son about aggressive women. Over and over he kept saying, "Listen, my son. Hear my warnings. Embrace what I say, because it's important."

The writer concludes the passage by saying, *"Don't fool around with her, Son. Don't go near her. Because she runs a halfway house to hell, and she has your grave clothes and your coffin, Son. Heads up. This is dangerous stuff we're talking about here"* (my paraphrase of Proverbs 7:24-27).

Here's one other Scripture your son should be familiar with, and commit to memory:

> "Now flee from youthful lusts and pursue righteousness, faith, love and peace, with those who call on the Lord from a pure heart."
>
> **2 Timothy 2:22**

TRAINING YOUR DAUGHTERS

Now, how do you keep your daughters from being drawn into this culture of aggression and impropriety? If you are raising a daughter, there are at least four things you should consider.

1. Equip your daughter with a biblical, healthy, God-centred perspective of her sexuality. She needs to understand how her clothes and her behaviour affect boys. When girls are too flirty or too friendly with the opposite sex, they need to be told. If you witness this kind of behaviour, rehearse it and relive it later on and talk about what it does to guys. Explain what is appropriate in terms of a friendly relationship between a young lady and a young man. This needs to be done without being rude, but we cannot let our daughters get away with being overly friendly or overly aggressive.

2. As a mother, you should model what you teach your daughters. Dress appropriately, in the way you would want your teenage daughter to dress when they grow older. A mother sends mixed signals when she tells her daughter to dress conservatively, but her own clothes call too much attention to her body.

3. Dads, actively love your daughters. Give your daughter words of affection, warm hugs, and gentle kisses that let her know that she's sweet, she is your daughter, and no matter how big she gets, you are never going to stop giving her those words and hugs. No matter how threatening that may be as your daughter matures, you need to let her know that there's a wholesome love through words and affection that occurs within a God-centred family.

4. Promptly correct inappropriate behaviour. Pray about how you instruct, help and correct your daughter. Train her as to what is appropriate and what is not. This could be everything from how she looks at guys, to the makeup she wears, to her choice of clothes.

One of the most important things I did with my aunt's daughters was to go shopping with them. It was important for two reasons: It showed me how difficult it was for them to find appropriate clothing that is modest and fashionable; and secondly, it allowed me to give my approval or disapproval before the purchase was made.

Whether you are a mum or dad, and whether you are raising boys or girls, your children need your love and guidance as never before. They need to be loved when they do not believe in themselves. They need to be clothed in wisdom that morally protects them like armour.

Always kiss your children goodnight,
even if they're already asleep

*- **H. Jackson Brown, Jr.***

17

Exercise, Fun and Play

As much as we care about our children's spiritual and psychological wellbeing, we cannot overlook their physical development. Exercise, sports and physical play come to the fore in this regard.

The ability of children to play, communicate and develop language is a fundamental part of their growth, which also impacts greatly on their overall development. Some children struggle to develop these skills and others develop them naturally at a later stage or through the help of adult interaction.

Play is considered an important part of children's wellbeing and development. The United Nations Convention on the Rights Of the Child (1989) (UNCRC) Article 31 emphasised that play is a fundamental right for all children and Article 13 also talks about children's right to freedom of expression (Lansdown, 2009). Play, communication and language underpins the (Early Years Foundation Stage) learning and all aspects of children's development (DfE 2014).

Kids who are active will:

♦ Have stronger muscles and bones.

♦ Have a leaner body because exercise helps control body fat.

♦ Be less likely to become overweight.

♦ Decrease the risk of developing Type 2 diabetes

♦ Lower blood pressure and blood cholesterol levels.

♦ Have a better outlook on life.

Being physically active every day is important for the healthy growth and development of babies, toddlers and pre-schoolers.

Babies

Babies should be encouraged to be active throughout the day, every day. Before your baby begins to crawl, encourage them to be physically active by reaching and grasping, pulling and pushing, moving their head, body and limbs during daily routines, and during supervised floor play, including tummy time. Once babies can move around, encourage them to be as active as possible in a safe, supervised and nurturing play environment.

Toddlers

Children who can walk on their own should be physically active every day for at least 180 minutes (three hours). This should be spread throughout the day, indoors or outside. The 180 minutes can include light activity such as standing up, moving around, rolling and playing, as well as more energetic activity like skipping, hopping, running and jumping. Active play, such as using a climbing frame, riding a bike, playing in water, chasing games and ball games, is the best way for this age group to get moving.

Children under five

Children under five should not be inactive for long periods, except when they're asleep. Watching TV, travelling by car, bus or train, or being strapped into a buggy for long periods are not good for a child's health and development. There's growing evidence that such behaviour can increase their risk of poor health.

KINDS OF ACTIVITIES

Moderate Activity

Examples of activities that require moderate effort for most young people include:

♦   Walking to school

♦   Playing in the playground

♦   Riding a scooter

♦   Skateboarding

♦   Rollerblading

♦   Walking the dog

♦   Cycling on level ground or ground with few hills

Moderate activity raises your heart rate and makes you sweat. One way to tell if you're working at a moderate level is if you can still talk, but you can't sing the words to a song.

Vigorous activity

Vigorous activity is linked to better general health, stronger bones and muscles, as well as higher levels of self-esteem.

There is good evidence vigorous activity can bring health benefits over and above that of moderate activity. A rule of thumb is that one minute of vigorous activity provides the same health benefits as two minutes of moderate activity.

Examples of activities that require vigorous effort for most young people include:

- Playing chase
- Energetic dancing
- Swimming
- Running
- Gymnastics
- Football
- Rugby
- Martial arts, such as karate
- Cycling fast or on hilly terrain

What counts as *light activity* for children? This would include a range of activities, such as:

- Standing up
- Moving around
- Walking
- Less energetic play

What counts as *energetic activity* for children? Examples of *energetic activities* suitable for most children who can walk on their own include:

♦   Active play (such as hide and seek and stuck in the mud)

♦   Running around

♦   Jumping on a trampoline

♦   Riding a bike

♦   Dancing

♦   Swimming

♦   Climbing

♦   Skipping rope

♦   Gymnastics

Energetic activity for children will make kids "huff and puff" and can include organised activities, such as dance and gymnastics. Any sort of active play will usually include bursts of energetic activity.

NUTRITIONAL NEEDS

To aid their physiological development, we need to ensure our children eat healthy meals. Eating balanced diets should become a lifestyle. Encourage your seeds to take fruits and smoothies (even teenagers need a balanced diet to aid their growth and keep them healthy).

When we emphasise healthy eating habits very early in our children's lives, we aid their growth physically, academically (yes, food helps in this area too) and spiritually. Those who learn to exercise self-control and not become gluttons, are more likely to keep the discipline throughout their adult life.

I highly recommend *Kids Recipe for Busy Mums,* an excellent book by Tracey Sokoya. You will find it is easy and quick to make these recipes.

Loving a child doesn't mean giving in to all his whims; to love him is to bring out the best in him, to teach him to love what is difficult

- Nadia Boulanger

18

The Power of Mentorship

A mentor, simply put, is an experienced, trusted person or trainer who has been where one would like to be. By looking up to and learning directly from such a person, a mentoring relationship is struck.

The concept of mentoring is as old as the book of Deuteronomy in the Old Testament. In the following passage, God provided a biblical format for mentoring within the family to ensure that faith in the one and living God would be passed from generation to generation.

> "Hear, O Israel: The Lord our God, the Lord is one. Love the Lord your God with all your heart and with all your soul and

with all your strength. These commandments that I give you today are to be on your hearts. Impress them on your children. Talk about them when you sit at home and when you walk along the road, when you lie down and when you get up. Tie them as symbols on your hands and bind them on your foreheads. Write them on the doorframes of your houses and on your gates."

Deuteronomy 6:4-9

Relationships are the primary means God established for learning about and preserving His commandments. Family relationships is central to this, particularly the relationship between parents and their children. With more years of experience in life, parents have the responsibility to impress God's ways on the children.

Unfortunately, close relationships are often lacking in today's society and family relationships are also breaking down. Effective mentoring relationships is able to bridge this gap as the more experienced pass on their knowledge to their mentees.

"Two are better than one, because they have a good return for their labour: If either of them falls down, one can help the other up. But pity anyone who falls and has no one to help them up."

Ecclesiastes 4:9-10

"As iron sharpens iron, so one person sharpens another."

Proverbs 27:17

"I myself am convinced, my brothers and sisters, that you yourselves are full of goodness, filled with knowledge and competent to instruct one another."

Romans 15:14

"And let us consider how we may spur one another on toward love and good deeds, not giving up meeting together, as some are in the habit of doing, but encouraging one another — and all the more as you see the Day approaching."

Hebrews 10:24-25

"Whatever you have learned or received or heard from me, or seen in me — put it into practice. And the God of peace will be with you."

Philippians 4:9

A mentoring relationship can exist between people on different levels:

- Younger to older

- Peer to peer

- Older to younger

Even though the term "mentor" is not in the Bible, there are many instances where someone who is wiser and more experienced in the ways of the Lord acts as a mentor to someone younger or newer in the faith.

Jethro, Moses' father-in-law, acted as a mentor to Moses after observing Moses' attempts to solve disputes among the Israelites (Exodus 18).

Early in the wilderness journey, Moses began to mentor Joshua. Years later, God chose Joshua to be the next leader of the Israelites because he had Moses' spirit and had been mentored for the leadership position (Deuteronomy 31,34).

Elisha was prepared for his prophetic ministry through his close relationship with the prophet Elijah. When Elijah was taken up into heaven, his mantel fell on Elisha and he received a double portion of his mentor's spirit (1 Kings 19; 2 Kings 2).

The Book of Ruth portrays Naomi as a mentor to Ruth, her Moabite daughter-in-law.

Ruth had such a strong relationship with Naomi that she refused to leave her for any reason. Naomi helped Ruth understand the laws and customs of the Israelites (Ruth 1-4).

Elizabeth, the mother of John the Baptist, mentored Mary after she learned she was to be the mother of Jesus. Elizabeth, being filled with the Holy Spirit, reaffirmed the work of God in Mary's life (Luke 1).

Barnabas was a mentor to Paul when he was a new Christian. Later they were sent as missionaries into Cyprus. The apostle Paul became a great spiritual leader and authored 14 books of the New Testament (Acts 4, 9 & 11).

Paul was a mentor to Timothy and described the young man as being "like-minded" with him in his commitment to serving God. Their relationship was so strong that Paul called it a father-son relationship (Acts 16; Philippians 2; 1 & 2 Timothy).

WHY MENTORSHIP?

♦ Mentors help their mentees to look to the Bible for answers. God's Word is our spiritual nourishment and it provides wisdom on every aspect of life.

- Mentees may view seeking advice as a sign of weakness. But mentors are prepared to offer insights and point out alternatives, while remembering that mentees must ultimately make their own decisions.

- Most importantly, mentors show their mentees that God is the ultimate, most significant source of wise counsel.

Mentoring is very vital in a child's life and parents should seek to encourage suitable mentoring relationship for their children. The presence of a mentor in a child's life can assure parents that the child will be adequately nurtured. This has worked well in the lives of my children.

While writing this book, I spoke to some mothers who all echoed the importance of mentors in their children's lives. One mother, for instance, described how her young son, called "T", was being mentored by "Big T" - he always goes to him for help and questions whenever he is disturbed. The mother knows "Big T" very well and has chosen him to be a mentor for "Young T."

I also remember a conversation I once had with Champion. "Mum," he said "you know, when I am upset, I just call D or M and talk to either of them. This has been a big help to me."

I was not even aware that he was doing this! Now this is very powerful, because D and M are 4 years older than Champion and, knowing them very well, they are good examples for Champion to follow.

Champion has mentors for character, academic and career development. These are people he would love to emulate. Although he knows that he is unique, yet he has mentees who he speaks to and even buys something out of his pocket money for when they are good and this is because his mentors do the same. This helps our seeds to be accountable and responsible too.

An old saying speaks to the art of mentoring: "Tell me, and I will forget. Show me, and I will remember. Involve me, and I will understand." Effective mentors do not have all the answers. Instead, they walk with their mentees through the process of discovering all the blessings and benefits of hearing and obeying God. (Author Unknown)

I have found the best way to give advice to your children is to find out what they want and then advise them to do it

- Harry S. Truman

19

Equip them for the

Real World

It is amazing how some parents protect their children like eggs that must not be broken. However, parents who are realists would prepare their seeds for the real world.

Due to overprotection, many parents are not teaching their children about the dangers of the world we live in. Children are not being empowered with the knowledge and skills they need to thrive in an ungodly world. Rather than keep them under "lock and key," we need to equip children with the right values. They should understand the implications of where they go, what they do, the clothes they wear, the associations they keep, what they see and hear, the social media activities they engage in, the apps they have on their gadget, sleepovers etc.

Parents, arise! There is a lot going on in the world! We must give our children the right foundation and place them in Abba's hands (spiritual side of things); we must also, as their custodians, give them the right foundation for social engagement. We need to show them unconditional love and let them know they are always loved at home (the place where charity starts). I have seen children, desperate for love and attention, go out there and do silly things - just because they are not loved at home. Please do not mistake "love and acceptance" for money, gadgets, clothes and the things that money can buy; what children need is quality time with their carers and nurturers.

Ironically, babies learn by experience that it is not all the time they cry that they get their parent's attention. In the real world, parents have to engage in other things at different times. This is especially true for mums who need to go back to work and have to put their babies in a nursery. For a time, it was just mummy and baby, but when reality kicks in, the toddler understands that mummy has to go somewhere and come back later. Even if they cry and throw tantrums, mummy will not say, "I love my child so much! If I go out I am letting my child down. So, I will stay with you forever!" No. Mummy knows that her toddler will soon settle in and begin to love it afterwards. This inevitable "me" time is healthy for both sides. The baby or toddler is now in the midst of his or her peers, which helps development, and mum gets to do what she wants to do too. Happy days!

We should always do whatever is right for the family, especially for the sake of preparing a child for the real world. Let them know that the time would come when they would need to step up and make independent choices in the real world. Although we would be there to guide them and hold their hands along the journey of life, they will also make mistakes and learn from their mistakes.

In a real world, you cannot give your children everything they desire just because you love them. On the contrary, you should explain the reasons why they cannot have some things. Learn to use the word NO or WAIT. It would teach them how to delay gratification.

John Rosemond put it this way: "Is your child getting enough vitamin "N" (N meaning

"No")? It does wonders for a child's well-being!

*Children are educated by what the grown-up
is and not by his talk*

- Carl Jung

20

Money and Delayed Gratification

The subject of money is seldom taught in the home. However, as parents, we must help our children become money-literate as this is an indispensable aspect of life. The truth is, many adults do not have a clue as to how money work! Given how important financial skills are to navigating life, it is equally surprising that our schools do not teach children about money.

Parents need a change of attitude in this area. We need to be proactive in passing financial education to our children. Take every opportunity to sow seeds of financial knowledge in your children. Teach them never to say "It's only £2!" Let them know that every penny matters and should be accounted for.

I started teaching my first about finances as soon as he was old enough to go to the shops. When I gave him money for an item, I would ask him how much the change would be. When he got older (about 10 years) I sent him to the supermarket, I would ask him why he got the buy-one-get-one-free item instead of the buy-one-get-one-half-price. He would explain to me that one free item is better than one that is half the price. I will then explain to him that this is not the case all the time; that it depends on whether you are in need of the thing in the first place, what the expiry date was (if it was a perishable item) etc.

I remember one day he came home with incorrect change. I had to send him back because before he got the change, he should have calculated how much his change would be. This also reinforced his mathematics ability.

Now that he is older and collects pocket money, he understands that he cannot come to me for a new pair of trainers until he has saved towards it, no matter how little the saving. This helps him to value what he has and appreciate when he receives a monetary gift from others. He knows that people worked hard for the money! Now, he gladly does things like mowing the garden, washing my car in exchange for a token payment (between £1 and £5!). As these are not his regular chores, he's happy to do some work for a fee!

Champion now asks me questions like, "Why do people use credit cards on things that are not essential instead of saving for them?" He would save up for our birthdays and wedding anniversaries (even £5 gifts sometimes) we truly appreciate it. Champion would not buy anything full price. He know how to search for a bargain! He does his research before asking if we could buy an item, with a full report of where to get what and at what price! It really pays to teach our children about finances from an early age.

FINANCIAL LESSONS FOR ALL AGES

Below are examples of some top money lessons you should endeavour to teach your children as they transition from toddler to young adult.

♦   *Ages 3-5:* You may have to wait to buy something you want.

- *Ages 6-10:* You need to make choices about how to spend money.

- *Ages 11-13:* The sooner you save, the faster your money can grow from compound interest.

- *Ages 14-18:* When comparing colleges, be sure to consider how much each school would cost.

- *Ages 18+:* You should use a credit card only if you can pay the balance off in full each month.

Don't handicap your children by making their lives easy

- Robert A. Heinlein

21

Reward and Punishment

As parents, we have the responsibility to train our children in the way of the Lord and to prepare them for a successful future. Inevitably, this would involve discipline and correction. When disciplining a child, however, we should consider it as a rescue mission; a mission of love to catch our children from the dangers that come from being outside God's protective rules for their life.

This being the case, it is important that we do not discipline our children in anger. Instead, remind them that they are loved and accepted. Disciple them when you have to and reassure them of the relationship you have with them and them with you (I am still learning these principles in my work with my children too).

Pastor and parent, Tedd Tripp, offers principles, applications, and advice on how to win a child's heart through care, instruction, discipleship, and discipline. One of the basic principles of his book, Shepherding a Child's Heart, is that every action of a child is a manifestation of his heart. If a child's behaviour is unruly or rebellious, then the actions themselves should most certainly be addressed - but only as a symptom of a greater disease.

I think Mr. Tripp did a splendid job of balancing discipleship - focusing on and addressing the heart reasons for a child's actions, and discipline - correcting the outward actions of a child. I also agreed with his analysis of what discipline really is; not revenge, or a chance for a parent to let out his anger, but a demonstration of love.

Our efforts as parents should not be directed towards changing our children's behaviour, but towards changing their hearts. It is pointless to aim for the appearance of godliness; instead we want to teach and train them to see the sin in their action and draw them to repentance.

As a father, the best way to love your children is to love their mother (and as a mother, their father). The quality of your marriage greatly affects the way you relate to your children and the way they receive love. If your marriage is healthy - both partners treating each other with kindness, respect, and integrity - you and your spouse will feel and act as partners in parenting."

As you discipline your children, be aware of and sensitive to their different personalities. It is important you understand their various love languages. (I highly recommend the book *The Five Love Languages of Children*, by Gary Chapman).

According to Gary Chapman, your children's primary love language falls under one of these:

- Physical Touch
- Words of Affirmation
- Quality Time
- Gifts
- Acts of Service

You should discover and speak your child's love language in dozens of ways! (see the test in the appendix section).

- Use the love languages to help your child learn best
- Discipline and correct more lovingly and effectively

Children are the living messages we send to a time we will not see

- Neil Postman

22

Rest

I love this definition of rest: "To cease work or movement in order to relax, sleep, or *recover strength.*" It is important we help our children to recover strength. Most of the time, children do not like to rest and some even see it as punishment. However, as a parent, you need to help your child imbibe the habit of recovering strength.

My Princess does not like this at all! Notwithstanding, whenever I see her unsettled, I know it is time for her body to replenish itself and I tell her to go to bed. Her immediate response is always "No." But I get firm, give her a bath and send her to sleep. Literally, she is fast asleep within ten minutes! She thereafter wakes up refreshed and renewed.

WHY CHILDREN NEED REST

The average kid has a busy day. There is school, homework, extra-curricular activities, including sports and clubs etc. By the end of the day, their body needs a break. Sleep allows their body to rest for the next day.

Everything that is alive needs sleep to survive. Even dogs and cat curl up for naps. Animals sleep for the same reason you do - to give their bodies a tiny vacation.

The body and brain needs sleep. Although no one is exactly sure what work the brain does when humans sleep, some scientists think that the brain sorts through and stores information, replaces chemicals, and solves problems while they snooze.

Most children between five and twelve get about 9.5 hours a night, but experts agree that most need ten or eleven hours each night. Sleep is an individual thing and some kids need more sleep than others.

When the body does not have enough hours to rest, it may feel tired or cranky, or may be unable to think clearly. Some might have a hard time following directions or instructions, or have an argument with you over something really stupid.

Another reason why are children need to get enough sleep is that without sleep, they will not grow as they should. Researchers believe too little sleep can affect growth and the immune system.

If we are to teach real peace in this world,
and if we are to carry on a real war against war,
we shall have to begin with the children

- Mahatma Gandhi

EPILOGUE

Nurturing

Through Prayer

The psalmist declared that *"Unless the Lord builds the house, the builders labour in vain"* (Psalm 127:1). This truth applies to everything in life, including the nurturing of our children. No matter how much effort we put into raising our children, without depending totally on God, our efforts will not bear the expected fruit. Prayer must undergird everything we do and our expectations would thus not be cut short.

Let us pray together:

Lord, help us as we continue on our parenting journey. I pray that we will be effective in helping our seeds to fulfil their destiny. May their hearts continue to yearn for You, in Jesus' name.

We thank You for counting us worthy to look after these special ones.

We ask that You give us the grace and strength to finish this journey well.

We ask that You give us the resources to equip them with Your word and the wisdom to answer the questions that they may ask.

We pray that our children have the will to say NO to the evil one and to stand up against peer pressure in Jesus' name.

We pray that their eyes will see Your goodness, their ears will hear Your goodness, their mouths will taste Your goodness and their minds will conceive Your goodness, in Jesus' name.

We ask that Your love will dwell in them and radiate to the world through them in Jesus' name, amen.

PARENTS PRAYING DAILY GUIDE

Monday

Ask God to place a protective, solid hedge around your children so that the devil would not be able to reach them and lead them into temptation (2 Thessalonians 3:3; Psalm 33:20).

Tuesday

Pray that your children would use godly wisdom in selecting friends and peers that will make a positive difference in their lives. Ask God to give each child a discernment of people as well as knowing the difference between right and wrong (Proverbs 1:10; 18:24; Deuteronomy 13:6,8).

Wednesday

Pray that your children would stay pure in their thoughts and deeds (Psalm 24:4-5; Job 17:9).

Thursday

Pray that the Holy Spirit convicts them if they wander into cheating, lies, or mischief (Hebrews 13:18-19).

Friday

Pray that your children will be alert and clear-minded as they attend school and extra-curricular activities, and as they take exams. Ask God to help them to remain motivated to do the best they are capable of doing (Colossians 3:17; 1 Corinthians 10:31).

Saturday

Pray for the spouse each child will marry someday. Ask God that they will come from godly homes and have an appetite to live the spiritual truths they have learned. Pray also that their goals and purpose will be compatible with your children's and their future homes would be godly (Deuteronomy 5:29).

Sunday

Ask God to help them live their lives for Him and that He will use them as a testimony and witness for His glory. Pray that they would grow to full spiritual maturity (Psalms 78:1-8, 103:17-18; Isaiah 54:13; Ephesians 3:20-21).

Children are our most valuable natural resource

- Herbert Hoover

SUGGESTED DEVOTIONALS

- *Keys for kids* (for children)
- *Wisdom Devotionals* (for teenagers)

EDUCATIONAL RESOURCES

- Children's Education in the UK (Grammar and Independent Schools)
- Russell Group Universities
- Pastor Nicholas Nunayon has been a blessing to me and my seeds. If you want to know more, please contact him on the following media:

Facebook: Pastor Nicholas Nunayon

Website: www.kingsgenfoundation.org

REFERENCES

Encouraging Words, Amy McCready

Available from: www.positiveparentingsolutions.com/
parenting/encouraging-words [Accessed 25/01/2017]

Knowing Jesus

Available from: www.bible.knowing-jesus.com/
topics/Parents-Duty-To-Children [Accessed
25/01/2017]

Seeds of Greatness, Cinde Lucas, Overflow Ministries

Available from: www.christianity.com/christian-life/
seeds-of-greatness-11551166.html [Accessed
25/01/2017]

How many times did Thomas Alva Edison fail exactly?

100 or 10000... anybody know exact figure?

Available from: www.quora.com/How-many-times-
did-Thomas-Alva-Edison-fail-exactly [Accessed
25/01/2017]

*15 Things Children Can (and Should) Value More Than
Possessions,* Joshua Becker

Available from: www.becomingminimalist.com/15-
things-children-can-and-should-value-more-than-
possessions/ [Accessed 25/01/2017]

Keep it simple

Available from: www.google.co.uk/webhp? sourceid=chrome-instant&ion=1&espv=2&ie=UTF-8#q=kiss+keep+it+simple [Accessed 25/01/2017]

Physical activity

Available from: www.nhs.uk/Livewell/fitness/Pages/physical-activity-guidelines-for-children.aspx [Accessed 26/01/2017]

N.H.S

11/07/2015

Available from: http://www.nhs.uk/Livewell/fitness/Pages/physical-activity-guidelines-for-young-people.aspx [Accessed 27/01/2017]

Biblical Basis for Mentoring

N.D

Available from: https://www.prisonfellowship.org/resources/training-resources/mentoring-ministry/ministry-basics/biblical-basis-for-mentoring/ [Accessed 27/01/2017]

John Rosemond

What I call Vitamin N − 'No' − can do wonders for a child's well-being

May 5, 2015 8:01 PM

Available from: http://www.kentucky.com/living/family/article44597919.html#storylink=cpy [Accessed 01/02/2017]

Melissa Edgington

January 31, 2017

Sex Education Should Start in the Christian Home

Available from: www. churchleaders.com/youth/youth-leaders-articles/298541-sex-education-start-christian-home-melissa-edgington.html?utm_source=youth-weekly-nl&utm_medium=email&utm_content=featured-image&utm_campaign=youth-weekly-nl&maropost_id=742195375&mpweb=256-2665981-742195375

Mind Power

Available from: www.exposingtruth.com/mind-power/ [Accessed 10/02/2017]

Forgetting

Available from: www.psychologistworld.com/memory/forgetting.php {Accessed 13/02/2017]

Positive Affirmations

Available from: www.makeavisionboard.com/positive-affirmations/ [Accessed 10/02/2017]

What is a Vision Board?

Available from: www.makeavisionboard.com/what-is-a-vision-board/ [Accessed 10/02/2017]

Is abstinence the goal?

Available from: www.familylife.com/articles/topics/parenting/challenges/sexual-purity/is-abstinence-the-goal [Accessed 10/02/2017]

Lessons to teach your kids

Available from: www.forbes.com/sites/laurashin/2013/10/15/the-5-most-important-money-lessons-to-teach-your-kids/#7414cd42498c [Accessed 10/02/2017]

Love Language Test

Available from: www.uen.org/cte/facs_cabinet/downloads/AdultRoles/S3O1**LoveLanguageTest.doc** Accessed 10/02/2017]

Erin Woodfin

How to Help Your Kids Fall Deeper in Love with God

Available from: www.churchleaders.com/youth/youth-leaders-articles/254302-get-kids-fall-deeper-love-god-created.html?utm_source=youth-weekly-nl&utm_medium=email&utm_content=text-link&utm_campaign=youth-weekly-nl&maropost_id=742195375&mpweb=256-2509998-742195375 [Accessed 14/02/2017]

Five Love Languages of Teenagers by Dr Gary Chapman (a noted marriage and family counsellor)

Northfield Publishing, Chicago (2000, 2005)

269 pages, including *The Five Love Languages Test for Teens*

ISBN-13: 978-1-881273-39-4

ISBN-10: 1-881273-39-3

(15/02/2017)

BOOKS

- *The Bible* (NIV and NKJV)
- *Shepherding a Child's Heart* by Tedd Tripp
- *The Five Love Languages of Children* by Gary Chapman, D. Ross Campbell
- *Kids Recipes for Busy Mums* by Tracey Sokoya

APPENDIX
THE FIVE LOVE LANGUAGES TEST
By Dr. Gary Chapman

Read each pair of statements and circle the one that best describes you.

1.   A.   I like to receive notes of affirmation from you.

       E.   I like it when you hug me.

2.   B.   I like to spend one-on-one time with you.

       D.   I feel loved when you give me practical help.

3.   C.   I like it when you give me gifts.

       B.   I like taking long walks with you.

4.   D.   I feel loved when you do things to help me.

       E.   I feel loved when you hug or touch me.

5.   E.   I feel loved when you hold me in your arms.

       C.   I feel loved when I receive a gift from you.

6. B. I like to go places with you.

    E. I like to hold hands with you.

7. A. I feel loved when you acknowledge me.

    C. Visible symbols of love (gifts) are very important to me.

8. E. I like to sit close to you.

    A. I like it when you tell me that I am attractive.

9. B. I like to spend time with you.

    C. I like to receive little gifts from you.

10. D. I know you love me when you help me.

    A. Your words of acceptance are important to me.

11. B. I like to be together when we do things.

    A. I like the kind words you say to me.

12. E. I feel whole when we hug.

    D. What you do affect me more than what you say.

13. A. I value your praise and try to avoid your criticism.

    C. Several inexpensive gifts mean more to me than one large expensive gift.

14. E. I feel closer to you when you touch me.

    B. I feel close when we are talking or doing something together.

15. A. I like you to compliment my achievements.

    D. I know you love me when you do things for me that you don't enjoy doing.

16. E. I like for you to touch me when you walk by.

    B. I like when you listen to me sympathetically.

17. C. I really enjoy receiving gifts from you.

    D. I feel loved when you help me with my home projects.

18. A. I like when you compliment my appearance.

    B. I feel loved when you take the time to understand my feelings.

19. E.   I feel secure when you are touching me.

    D.   Your acts of service make me feel loved.

20. D.   I appreciate the many things you do for me.

    C.   I like receiving gifts that you make.

21. B.   I really enjoy the feeling I get when you give me your undivided attention.

    D.   I really enjoy the feeling I get when you do some act of service for me.

22. C.   I feel loved when you celebrate my birthday with a gift.

    A.   I feel loved when you celebrate my birthday with meaningful words (written or spoken.)

23. D.   I feel loved when you help me out with my chores.

    C.   I know you are thinking of me when you give me a gift.

24. C.   I appreciate it when you remember special days with a gift.

    B.   I appreciate it when you listen patiently and don't interrupt me.

25. B. I enjoy extended trips with you.

    D. I like to know that you are concerned enough to help me with my daily task.

26. E. Kissing me unexpectedly makes me feel loved.

    C. Giving me a gift for no occasion makes me feel loved.

27. A. I like to be told that you appreciate me.

    B. I like for you to look at me when we are talking.

28. C. Your gifts are always special to me.

    E. I feel loved when you kiss me.

29. A. I feel loved when you tell me how much you appreciate me.

    D. I feel loved when you enthusiastically do a task I have requested.

30. E. I need to be hugged by you every day.

    A. I need your words of affirmation daily.

Add Total Number of Answers Here:

A. ـــــ Words of Affirmation

B. ـــــ Quality Time

C. ـــــ Receiving Gifts

D. ـــــ Acts of Service

E. ـــــ Physical Touch